In Loving Memory

Of
Theresa Panial
Lasinski
Mother
Of
Debborah Lutton
By
Blairsville Saltsburg
Education Association

BILL MAZEROSKI

BRIAN GILES

RALPH KINER

PAUL WANER

HONUS WAGNER

BARRY BONDS

PIE TRAYNOR

ARKY VAUGHAN

MAX CAREY

JASON KENDALL

WILLIE STARGELL

ROBERTO CLEMENTE

THE HISTORY OF THE
PITTSBURGH
PIRATES

WAYNE STEWART

CREATIVE 🍎 EDUCATION

Published by Creative Education, 123 South Broad Street, Mankato, MN 56001

Creative Education is an imprint of The Creative Company.

Designed by Rita Marshall.

Photographs by AllSport (Otto Greule), Associated Press/Wide World Photos,

Icon Sports Media (John McDonough, Chuck Solomon), Diane Johnson, SportsChrome

(Jeff Carlick, Rob Tringali Jr., Michael Zito), TimePix (Art Rickerby, George Tiedemann)

Library of Congress Cataloging-in-Publication Data

Stewart, Wayne, 1951- The history of the Pittsburgh Pirates / by Wayne Stewart.

p. cm. — (Baseball)   ISBN 978-1-58341-220-6

Summary: A team history of the Pittsburgh Pirates, who have been playing baseball

since the 1880s.

1. Pittsburgh Pirates (Baseball team)—History—

Juvenile literature. [1. Pittsburgh Pirates (Baseball team)—History.

2. Baseball—History.] I. Title. II. Baseball (Mankato, Minn.).

GV875.P5 S84 2002   796.357'64'0974886—dc21   2001047870

9 8 7 6 5 4 3 2

PITTSBURGH,

PENNSYLVANIA, IS A HARDWORKING COMMUNITY

known as the "Steel City" because of its numerous steel mills. The city is interesting geographically in that it was built at the intersection of three major rivers. The location where two rivers join to form the Ohio River is called the Golden Triangle and is at the heart of the city's downtown area.

Since the late 1880s, Pittsburgh has been home to a professional baseball team called the Pirates (so-named because the club was known to steal talented players away from other teams in its early days), who played many of their seasons in a ballpark fittingly named Three Rivers Stadium. Over the years, the Pirates have usually mirrored the character of Pittsburgh, earning a reputation

FRED CLARKE

for their hard-nosed and unselfish style of play.

{WAY BACK WHEN} Pittsburgh became a member of the

National League (NL) in 1887. The Pirates finished

higher than fifth place only once in the 19th century,

but they sailed high in 1900, finishing in second place.

Then, from 1901 to 1903, the Pirates captured three

straight NL pennants.

The Pirates soared to their finest mark in team history in **1902**, going a stunning 103–36.

6   Responsible for this turnaround were such stars as pitcher

Deacon Phillippe, outfielder/manager Fred Clarke, and shortstop

Honus Wagner. Wagner became the greatest of the bunch, earning a

total of eight batting titles and becoming the first member of

baseball's prestigious 3,000-hit club. The broad-shouldered

shortstop had bowed legs that made him appear unathletic, but he

was an astounding player. As one reporter wrote, "He walks like a

crab, fields like an octopus, and hits like the devil."

DEACON   PHILLIPPE

Honus Wagner, the "Flying Dutchman," posted a career .329 batting average.

HONUS WAGNER

There was no World Series in 1901 or 1902, but in 1903, the Pirates challenged the American League champion Boston Pilgrims for the right to be called world champions. Phillippe topped Boston's ace, Cy Young, in the first game of the best-of-nine series. However, Boston then pulled away to win the first World Series.

In 1909, Pittsburgh returned to the World Series after winning a club-record 110 games. The series that year was billed as a marquee matchup between Wagner and Detroit Tigers outfielder Ty Cobb. But the real star of the World Series was Pittsburgh pitcher Babe Adams. Known for his fine control, Adams baffled the Tigers' hitters, winning three games as the Pirates captured the championship.

{PIE AND "POISON"} For the most part, the Pirates were a respectable team from 1910 to 1925, led by such standouts as

Pitcher Howie Camnitz put together a 1.56 ERA in **1908**, setting a team record that still stands.

HOWIE CAMNITZ

The Pirates have long been known for their quick and aggressive style.

TONY WOMACK

infielder Pie Traynor. One of only nine third basemen to be elected

to the Hall of Fame, Traynor was equally skilled at the plate and in

In **1921**, a Pittsburgh versus Philadelphia game was the first ever broadcast over the radio.

the field. "If I were to pick the greatest team player in

baseball today—and I have some of the greats on my

own club—I would have to pick Pie Traynor," said

John McGraw, the legendary manager of the New

York Giants.

In the early 1920s, Pittsburgh also featured speedy outfielders

Kiki Cuyler and Max Carey. Cuyler was a defensive standout who was

said to be the fastest major-league player of the 1920s. Carey, who

tracked down fly balls with an easy, gliding stride, led the NL in steals

10 times. In 1922, he stole bases almost at will, coming up with 51

steals and getting caught just twice!

In 1925, Pittsburgh finally returned to the top. That year, it

captured the NL flag and then overcame a sluggish start against the

THE WANERS

Washington Senators to win the World Series. In doing so, the

Pirates became the first team ever to come back from a three-

games-to-one World Series deficit.

Two years later, the Pirates were armed with a deadly new

outfield duo: brothers Paul and Lloyd Waner. Paul, known as "Big

Poison," hit a league-leading .380 and won the NL Most Valuable

Player (MVP) award in 1927. Naturally, his younger brother Lloyd

was called "Little Poison." Lloyd, a slap hitter with great speed,

Sensational
outfielder
Paul Waner
propelled the
Pirates to
the **1927**
World Series
with 131 RBI.collected 223 hits in 1927, an NL record for hits in a

season by a rookie. "They can run like scalded cats,"

said one opposing big-league manager. "They spray the

ball all over the field and are really tough to defend."

The "Poisons" led the Pirates back to the World Series

14 in 1927, where they faced the New York Yankees and their famous

"Murderers' Row" lineup. Some say Pittsburgh was doomed even

before the first pitch was fired. Legend has it that the Pirates

became intimidated when they watched Babe Ruth and other

Yankees sluggers crush ball after ball out of the park during batting

practice. The Yankees won the series in four straight games.

{PIRATES WALK THE PLANK} After 1927, the Pirates' plun-

dering days were over for quite some time. In fact, they wouldn't

BARRY BONDS

win another NL flag for 33 years. Still, some new stars emerged in

the Steel City to brighten this otherwise dark era. One such player

was shortstop Arky Vaughan. Vaughan was quiet by nature, but his

accomplishments on the field and at the plate spoke volumes. In

each of his 10 seasons with the Pirates (1932 to 1941), he never hit

below the .300 mark. He was also a slick fielder and a fine base runner.

Next came outfielder Ralph Kiner, a swashbuckling power hitter. From 1947 to 1949, he hit a combined 145 home runs, and from 1946 to 1952, he won seven straight home run crowns—a feat no other major-league player has ever matched. Unfortunately, a back ailment limited Kiner's career to 10 seasons, preventing him from shattering even more home run records.

Over the course of his great career, Ralph Kiner averaged one home run per every 14 at-bats.

The Pirates fielded some terrible teams in the early 1950s. From 1952 to 1955, Pittsburgh not only finished in last place each season, but it averaged a whopping 103 losses per season. The team remained in the NL cellar despite the efforts of powerful first baseman Dick Stuart, center fielder Bill Virdon, and brilliant relief pitcher Roy Face. Face was known for his baffling forkball, which was prone to flutter in nearly any direction. In 1959, the ace reliever went 18–1, but the Pirates still struggled.

RALPH KINER

The Pirates
have been
entertaining
Pittsburgh
fans for
more than
115 years.

{BEAT 'EM BUCS} Suddenly, in 1960, Pittsburgh's luck changed. The 1960 season was a magical campaign in which every-thing seemed to go right for the Pirates. Fans adopted the battle cry "Beat 'em Bucs," and the Pirates did just that.

Forty-one years after his famous home run, Bill Mazeroski would be elected to the Hall of Fame.

The team tore to a 95–59 record, thanks largely to Roberto Clemente, the Pirates' young right fielder. An intensely proud man, Clemente could do it all. Over the course of his career, he would earn 12 Gold Glove awards and lead the NL in batting four times. "The big thing about Clemente," praised San Francisco Giants pitcher Juan Marichal, "is that he can hit any pitch. I don't mean only strikes. He can hit a ball off his ankles or off his ear."

Other standouts on that 1960 team were pitcher Vernon Law, shortstop Dick Groat, and second baseman Bill Mazeroski. Law won

BILL MAZEROSKI

20 games and the Cy Young Award, and Groat batted .325 and was

named NL MVP. Mazeroski, meanwhile, was a peerless defender

who astounded even teammates with his fielding heroics. "It was as

if his hands never touched the ball," said Groat. "As soon as the ball

reached his glove, it was on its way to first base. Frankly, I never saw

anything like it."

After winning the NL pennant, the Pirates capped their stunning

season by toppling the mighty New York Yankees in one of the most

Catcher Smoky Burgess was one of eight Pirates players named to the **1960** All-Star Game.

bizarre World Series ever. Even though the Yankees

won by scores of 16–3, 10–0, and 12–0 in three games

and outscored the Pirates by a total of 55–27 in the

series, Pittsburgh somehow prevailed, winning in

seven contests.

Clemente was brilliant in the World Series, but it was

Mazeroski who really stole the spotlight. Although he was primarily

known for his sure glove, in the final game of the series, he became

a hero with his bat. Entering the bottom of the ninth inning with

the game tied 9–9, "Maz" promptly hit a home run to become the

first player ever to clout a World Series-winning blast.

{THE GOLDEN '70s} Despite the efforts of Maz and

Clemente, the Pirates faded in the standings throughout the rest of

SMOKY BURGESS

Kent Tekulve emerged as Pittsburgh's top reliever in the late **1970s** and early **'80s**.

KENT TEKULVE

the 1960s. Once the team finally did reach the top again, however,

it stayed for a while. In the 1970s, Pittsburgh became a powerhouse,

winning the NL Eastern Division six times (the league

was split into two divisions in 1969).

Pittsburgh was led during that era by hard-hitting

outfielders Al Oliver and Willie "Pops" Stargell. In

1971, Stargell slammed 48 home runs, and the power-

ful Pirates breezed into the World Series. There, Clemente—still a

star late in his career—batted .414 to carry the Pirates to another

world championship.

Sadly, Clemente was killed in a plane crash just a year later

while flying to Central America on a charity mission. As the Pirates

mourned his tragic death, they continued to win games. Emerging as

the team's undisputed leader in the late '70s was Stargell, who by

then had moved to first base. In 1979, he was simply incredible,

Roberto Clemente got at least one hit in each of the 14 World Series games he played.

ROBERTO CLEMENTE

leading Pittsburgh to another world championship and earning

MVP honors in the regular season, the NL Championship Series

(NLCS), and the World Series. "I never saw anything like it. He

doesn't just hit pitchers. He takes away their dignity," said Los

Angeles Dodgers pitcher Don Sutton.

As great as Stargell was in 1979, he didn't win the World Series single-handedly. Making major contributions were catcher Manny Sanguillen and outfielder Dave Parker. Sanguillen was a renowned bad-ball hitter, while Parker was known for his long-ball power and boastful ways. "When the leaves turn brown," he said during the spring of each season, "I'll wear the batting crown."

Although the Pirates have always been known more for their hitters than their pitchers (by 2002, 12 Pirates players were enshrined in the Hall of Fame, but none were pitchers), relief pitcher Kent Tekulve played a key role in the Pirates' winning ways during the glorious '70s. Upon his retirement, the lanky sidewinder had appeared in more games than any major-league pitcher except former great Hoyt Wilhelm.

Willie Stargell hit more home runs (296) during the '70s than any other big-league player.

{THE PIRATES RISE...AND FALL} In the 1980s, the Pirates fell from prominence, managing only two second-place finishes

WILLIE STARGELL

behind such players as third baseman Bill Madlock and swift

outfielder Omar Moreno. It wasn't until the early 1990s that

A four-time
All-Star,
catcher
Tony Pena
was a much-
needed bright
spot in the
mid-**1980s**.

Pittsburgh emerged as a contender again, winning the

NL East in 1990, 1991, and 1992.

The player most responsible for the Pirates' resur-

gence was Barry Bonds. From 1986 through 1992, the

star outfielder was simply scintillating. In 1990, he hit

28 .300, smashed 33 home runs, and swiped 52 bases—numbers that

earned him the first of four career NL MVP awards. "He's the best

player in the game, and it's not even close," said Philadelphia Phillies

catcher Darren Daulton.

Outfielder Andy Van Slyke and third baseman Bobby Bonilla

also emerged as stars in the late 1980s and early '90s. Van Slyke was

a fine defensive player, but he also stood out at the plate, leading

the NL in hits in 1992. Next to Bonds, the burly Bonilla was the

TONY PENA

team's top run producer, driving in a combined 220 runs in 1990 and 1991. Unfortunately, despite this talent, the Pirates could not reach the World Series. By 1994, Bonds, Bonilla, and Van Slyke had all left Pittsburgh, and the Pirates went into a tailspin, posting losing records the rest of the decade.

As they battled for respect in the late 1990s, the Pirates brought in much-needed talent by signing hardworking catcher Jason Kendall and outfielder Brian Giles. Kendall was known for his toughness; in 1998, he was hit by a pitch a whopping 31 times. Giles, meanwhile, was a great hitter who batted .315 with 74 homers and 238 RBI in his first two seasons with Pittsburgh (1999 and 2000). Fans in the Steel City hoped that the duo—along with pitcher Todd Ritchie and slugging third baseman Aramis Ramirez—would lead Pittsburgh back to glory.

In **1991**, Bobby Bonilla drove in 120 runs, the most by a Pittsburgh player in 19 seasons.

BOBBY BONILLA

Renowned for his toughness, Jason Kendall was among the NL's elite catchers.

JASON KENDALL

Brian Giles led the team in RBI in **1999** and **2000**, posting at least 115 each year.

BRIAN GILES

In 2001, the Pirates left Three Rivers Stadium—their home of

30 years—and moved into the new PNC Park in downtown

Big things
were expected
of brawny
third baseman
Aramis
Ramirez in
2003 and
beyond.

Pittsburgh. In more than a century of baseball, the

Pirates have made Pittsburgh not only the city of

three rivers, but the city of five World Series titles

as well. As the 21st century unfolds, the Pirates

continue to sail the NL East seas in search of still

more championship trophies.

ARAMIS RAMIREZ